STOCK MARKET FUNDAMENTALS

STOCK MARKET FUNDAMENTALS

A BEGINNER'S GUIDE

COREY MACK

Corey Mack
Stock Market Fundamentals

Published by Spines

ISBN: 979-8-89950-650-5

Spines

CONTENTS

INTRODUCTION

The stock market can seem mysterious and intimidating to newcomers: flashing tickers, jargon-filled analysis, and endless charts. Yet at its core, it's simply a mechanism that allows you to own pieces of great companies and share in their growth.

In this book, you'll learn:

How the Market Works—from exchanges and indices to order types and settlement.

Getting Started—choosing a brokerage, placing your first trade, and setting realistic expectations.

Fundamental Analysis—reading financial statements, valuing companies, and spotting quality businesses.

Technical Analysis Basics—understanding price charts, trends, and common indicators.

Building Your Portfolio—diversification, asset allocation, and long-term vs. short-term strategies.

Risk Management & Psychology—controlling emotion, setting stop-losses, and maintaining discipline.

Whether you're saving for retirement, funding a major purchase, or simply curious about how stocks work, this guide will demystify each concept with clear explanations, real-world examples, and actionable steps. Let's turn that flashing ticker into your path toward financial confidence.

1 WHAT IS THE STOCK MARKET?

The stock market often evokes images of frantic trading floors, flashing tickers, and steep gains or losses. Yet beneath the surface volatility lies a well-structured, regulated mechanism that enables companies to raise capital and investors to own shares of those companies. In this chapter, we'll demystify the stock market by exploring:

- The fundamental purpose and functions of the market
- How stocks are created and issued
- The distinction between primary and secondary markets
- The role of exchanges and trading venues
- The key participants who drive supply, demand, and liquidity
- How major indices provide market benchmarks

1.1 THE STOCK MARKET'S PURPOSE

At its core, the stock market serves two primary functions:

Capital Formation for Companies (Primary Market)

Companies issue new shares to raise funds for growth, acquisitions, R&D, or debt reduction.

The initial sale of shares to the public—known as an Initial Public Offering (IPO)—transitions a private company into a publicly traded one.

Price Discovery & Liquidity for Investors (Secondary Market)

Once shares are issued, investors buy and sell existing stock among themselves.

This continuous trading establishes the market price for each company's shares through supply-and-demand dynamics.

Liquidity—the ability to buy or sell quickly at a transparent price—makes ownership of shares practical for individuals and institutions alike.

1.2 PRIMARY VS. SECONDARY MARKETS

1.2.1 Primary Market: Issuance of New Shares

Definition: Where companies raise fresh capital by issuing new securities.

Process:

- **Underwriting**: Investment banks assess the company's value, determine an offering price, and guarantee sale of shares to the public.
- **Regulatory Filings**: Companies file a registration statement (e.g., Form S-1 with the U.S. SEC) detailing business operations, financials, and risk factors.
- **Roadshow & Pricing**: Executives present to institutional investors; banks set the final IPO price based on demand.
- **Allocation**: Shares are allocated to institutional and retail investors at the IPO price.

Key Outcome: The company receives proceeds from the sale (minus underwriting fees), and new shares enter circulation.

1.2.2 Secondary Market: Trading Existing Shares

Definition: Where investors buy and sell shares with one another, and the issuing company is not directly involved.

Mechanics:

- **Orders**: Investors submit market, limit, or stop orders to buy or sell.
- **Matchmaking**: Exchanges or alternative trading systems (ATS) match buyers and sellers.
- **Settlement**: Trades typically settle in two business days (T+2), at which point ownership and funds exchange hands.

Key Benefit: Provides liquidity and a continuous price-discovery mechanism, allowing investors to adjust their holdings in response to new information or changing objectives.

1.3 HOW STOCKS ARE CREATED

Authorization

A corporation's charter (Articles of Incorporation) authorizes a certain number of shares.

Issuance

At IPO or subsequent secondary offerings, the board approves issuance of a portion of authorized shares.

Outstanding vs. Treasury Shares

- **Outstanding Shares:** Actively held by investors.
- **Treasury Shares:** Previously issued and later repurchased by the company; not entitled to dividends or voting rights.

1.4 STOCK EXCHANGES & TRADING VENUES

1.4.1 Traditional Exchanges

New York Stock Exchange (NYSE)

- **Market Model:** Auction-based, with designated market makers (DMMs) who facilitate orderly trading and price improvement.
- **Floor & Electronic:** Hybrid model combining human floor brokers with electronic matching.

NASDAQ

- **Market Model:** Fully electronic, with multiple market makers competing to post the best bid and ask quotations.
- **Tech Focus:** Historically home to many technology and growth companies.

1.4.2 Alternative Trading Systems (ATS)

Dark Pools

Private venues where large institutional orders execute without pre-trade transparency, reducing market impact.

Electronic Communication Networks (ECNs)

Automated systems that match buy and sell orders, often providing extended trading hours.

1.4.3 Over-the-Counter (OTC)

- **Definition:** Trading of securities not listed on formal exchanges.
- **Markets:** OTC Bulletin Board (OTCBB) and OTC Markets Group's tiers (OTCQX, OTCQB, Pink).
- **Participants:** Smaller or international companies that don't meet exchange listing standards.

1.5 MARKET PARTICIPANTS

Participant	Role & Motivation
Retail Investors	Individual traders and investors; seek capital appreciation, dividends, or income.
Institutional Investors	Mutual funds, pension funds, hedge funds; trade large blocks, influence liquidity.
Market Makers / DMMs	Provide continuous bids and offers, narrowing spreads, enhancing liquidity.
Brokers & Dealers	Execute orders on behalf of clients; some may also trade for their own accounts.
High-Frequency Traders	Employ algorithms to capitalize on very short-term price discrepancies.
Regulators (SEC, FINRA)	Enforce market rules, protect investors, ensure fair and orderly markets.

1.6 LIQUIDITY & PRICE DISCOVERY

Liquidity

- **Definition:** The ease with which an asset can be bought or sold without materially affecting its price.
- **Indicators:** Tight bid-ask spreads, high trading volume, depth of order book.

Price Discovery

- **Mechanism:** Continuous matching of buy and sell orders reveals the market consensus on a stock's value.
- **Drivers:** Company fundamentals, macroeconomic news, technical factors, and investor sentiment.

1.7 STOCK MARKET INDICES

Indices aggregate prices of select stocks to measure overall market or sector performance.

Index	Description	Composition
S&P 500	Broad U.S. large-cap benchmark	500 leading U.S. companies
Dow Jones Industrial Average (DJIA)	Price-weighted index of 30 blue-chip U.S. firms	30 large, established companies
NASDAQ Composite	Heavily tech-oriented, includes >3,000 stocks	All NASDAQ-listed securities
Russell 2000	Small-cap U.S. benchmark	2,000 smallest S&P Russell 3000 companies

Uses:

- **Benchmarking:** Compare portfolio returns against the market.
- **Market Sentiment:** Gauge bullish or bearish trends.
- **Product Basis:** Underlie index funds and ETFs for passive investing.

1.8 HOW TO READ A STOCK QUOTE

A typical stock quote includes:

Field	Explanation
Ticker Symbol	Abbreviation (e.g., AAPL, MSFT) representing the company.
Last Price	Most recent trade price.
Change / %	Price change and percentage since previous close.
Bid / Ask	Highest price buyers will pay / lowest price sellers ask.
Volume	Shares traded during the session.
52-Week High/Low	Highest and lowest prices over the past year.

1.9 KEY TAKEAWAYS

- **Dual Function:** The stock market both raises capital for companies (primary market) and provides liquidity and transparent pricing for investors (secondary market).
- **Exchanges & Venues:** From NYSE's floor to NASDAQ's electronic model and dark pools, trading occurs in multiple interconnected venues.
- **Diverse Participants:** Retail and institutional investors, market makers, and regulators each play distinct roles that contribute to liquidity and fairness.
- **Indices & Benchmarks:** Market gauges like the S&P 500 and DJIA distill broad market movements into actionable benchmarks.
- **Price Discovery & Liquidity:** Continuous order matching reveals the market price, while volume and spreads indicate how easily you can enter or exit positions.

With these fundamentals in place, you're now equipped to open your first brokerage account, understand order types, and place trades—topics we'll tackle in **Chapter 2: How to Get Started**.

2 HOW TO GET STARTED

Embarking on your investing journey begins with selecting the right brokerage, opening and funding your account, and understanding how to place your first trade. This chapter walks you step-by-step through that process, laying the groundwork for confident, well-informed investing.

2.1 CHOOSING A BROKERAGE ACCOUNT

Your brokerage is the gateway to the markets. Consider these factors when evaluating providers:

Criterion	Considerations
Cost Structure	Commissions per trade, per-share fees, account minimums, inactivity or platform fees.
Available Products	Stocks, ETFs, mutual funds, options, bonds, forex, crypto.
Platform & Tools	Ease of use, charting, screeners, mobile app, API access.
Research & Education	Analyst reports, model portfolios, educational articles, webinars.
Customer Service	Phone support, chat, dedicated rep, response times.
Account Types	Individual, joint, retirement (IRA/401(k)), custodial, margin-enabled.
Order Execution Quality	Speed, routing options, likelihood of price improvement.
Robo-Advisor Features	Automated portfolio construction and rebalancing, goal-setting interfaces.

2.1.1 Full-Service vs. Discount vs. Robo-Advisor

Full-Service Broker

Offers personalized advice, financial planning, and wealth management.

Fees are higher—typically a percentage of assets under management.

Discount Broker

Online platforms with low or zero commissions on stocks/ETFs.

You execute your own trades; access to research varies.

Robo-Advisor

Automated portfolio allocation based on your risk profile.

Low fees; limited customization; generally invests in broad-market ETFs.

Best Practice:

If you're a beginner planning to self-direct, start with a reputable discount broker offering robust educational resources and intuitive tools. Consider a robo-advisor if you prefer a hands-off, automated approach.

2.2 OPENING & FUNDING YOUR ACCOUNT

2.2.1 Account Application Process

Gather Documentation

Government-issued ID (driver's license or passport)

Social Security Number (SSN) or Tax ID

Proof of address (utility bill or lease)

Complete the Online Application

Personal information, employment, financial-status questions, investment experience.

Consent to margin or options privileges if desired (fills out a risk questionnaire).

Account Verification

Broker reviews your application; may request additional ID verification.

Approval typically takes 1–3 business days.

2.2.2 Funding Options

Method	Pros	Cons
Bank Transfer (ACH)	Free, easy, integrates with checking/savings.	May take 1–3 business days to clear.
Wire Transfer	Same-day funding (if initiated early).	Fees charged by banks ($10–$30).
Check Deposit	Familiar process.	Slow clearing (5–7 business days).
Brokerage Transfer (ACAT)	Moves assets from another broker directly.	May incur outbound fees; takes 3–7 business days.
Mobile Deposit	Convenient via app.	Subject to daily deposit limits and holds.

Tip: For your first trade, fund at least the amount needed for one or two small positions plus a buffer for fees or margin requirements.

2.3 UNDERSTANDING ORDER TYPES

Knowing which order type to use helps control execution price and timing. Below is an overview:

Order Type	Description	Pros	Cons
Market Order	Buy or sell immediately at the best available price.	Fast execution; ensures order fills.	Price uncertainty—may execute at worse price.
Limit Order	Sets a maximum (buy) or minimum (sell) price; executes only at that price or better.	Price control; avoid chasing market.	May not fill if price doesn't reach limit.
Stop Order	Becomes a market order once a trigger price is reached.	Protects profits or limits losses.	Triggered order may fill at unfavorable price slippage.
Stop-Limit Order	Becomes a limit order at trigger price; executes within specified limit bounds.	Combines stop discipline with price control.	May not fill if limit price isn't met post-trigger.
Trailing Stop	Trigger price adjusts by a specified percentage or dollar amount as market moves.	Locks in gains by "trailing" favorable moves.	Complexity; may trigger prematurely in volatile markets.

Example:

To buy XYZ shares only if they drop to $48: place a limit order at $48.

To sell ABC shares if they fall below $52: place a stop order with a trigger at $52.

2.4 PLACING YOUR FIRST TRADE

Follow these steps to execute your inaugural transaction:

Log In & Navigate

Access your broker's web or mobile platform; select "Trade" or "Buy/Sell."

Enter Ticker Symbol

Confirm the correct exchange listing (e.g., "AAPL" for Apple Inc. on NASDAQ).

Choose Action

"Buy" or "Sell," order type (market, limit, etc.), quantity of shares.

Set Price (if applicable)

For limit or stop orders, specify your desired price or trigger.

Review & Submit

Double-check all details—symbol, quantity, order type, and estimated cost.

Monitor Status

Track order status: "New," "Partially Filled," "Filled," or "Cancelled."

Confirm Execution

Receive trade confirmation via email or platform notification; note execution price and fees.

2.5 SETTLEMENT & POST-TRADE MANAGEMENT

Settlement Cycle (T+2):

Shares transfer and funds settle two business days after trade date.

Trade Confirmations:

Review daily statements for accuracy; file confirmations for tax and recordkeeping.

Position Monitoring:

Track your holdings, unrealized gains/losses, and account balance via your dashboard.

Margin Considerations:

If using margin, maintain required equity levels to avoid margin calls.

2.6 COMMON PITFALLS & HOW TO AVOID THEM

Pitfall	Prevention Strategy
Choosing Broker on Price Alone	Balance fees with platform reliability, research tools, and customer support.
Using Market Orders in Thinly Traded Stocks	Use limit orders to prevent large price slippage.
Over-Leveraging Margin	Understand margin interest rates, maintenance requirements, and potential for rapid losses.
Not Reviewing Trade Details Before Submission	Always perform a "second glance" on symbol, quantity, and order type to avoid fat-finger errors.
Ignoring Settlement Restrictions	Ensure sufficient settled cash before placing new trades or withdrawals to prevent rejections.
Failing to Keep Records	Archive trade confirmations and monthly statements for tax reporting and performance analysis.

2.7 BEST PRACTICES & RECOMMENDATIONS

Start Small: Place modest trades initially to learn platform mechanics and order execution nuances.

Use Practice (Paper-Trading) Accounts: Many brokers offer simulated trading to build confidence without risking capital.

Educate Continuously: Leverage broker-provided webinars, tutorials, and knowledge centers.

Maintain an Order Log: Record your rationale for each trade—entry, exit criteria, and outcome—to develop discipline and learn from experience.

Monitor One Market at a Time: Focus on a small number of stocks or ETFs until you master order types and settlement processes.

2.8 KEY TAKEAWAYS

Broker Selection Matters: Evaluate cost, tools, product offerings, and support to find the best fit for your style and goals.

Order Types Give Control: Use limit and stop orders to manage price risk; reserve market orders for highly liquid, large-cap stocks.

Process Discipline: Follow a consistent checklist for submitting trades, monitoring execution, and recording details.

Recordkeeping Is Essential: Accurate records aid in performance review, tax preparation, and regulatory compliance.

Continuous Learning: Treat your first trades as structured experiments —analyze outcomes, refine your approach, and build expertise.

With your account open, funded, and first trades executed, you're now ready to deepen your understanding of market participants and structure in **Chapter 3: Understanding Market Participants & Structure**.

3 UNDERSTANDING MARKET PARTICIPANTS & STRUCTURE

Behind every executed trade are a variety of actors and venues that together ensure the market operates smoothly, fairly, and with sufficient liquidity. In this chapter, we'll introduce the major participants, explain how trading venues and market structure work, and highlight the role regulatory bodies play in overseeing the ecosystem.

3.1 RETAIL INVESTORS VS. INSTITUTIONAL INVESTORS

3.1.1 Retail Investors

Definition: Individual traders and long-term buy-and-hold investors who trade in their personal accounts.

Characteristics:

- Smaller order sizes, typically tens to hundreds of shares per trade.
- Often guided by personal research, news sources, or financial advisors.
- May lack access to sophisticated order routing or dark-pool venues.

Impact:

- Retail volume can swing smaller-cap stocks and create noticeable volatility, especially in concentrated trades (e.g., "meme" stocks).

3.1.2 Institutional Investors

Definition: Large entities such as mutual funds, pension funds, hedge funds, insurance companies, and endowments.

Characteristics:

- Trade in blocks of thousands or even millions of shares.
- Employ professional research teams, quantitative models, and algorithmic strategies.
- Can negotiate lower trading fees and access special liquidity venues.

Impact:

- Provide substantial liquidity to the market.
- Their large orders can move prices; sophisticated traders use algorithms to slice orders into smaller pieces to minimize market impact.

3.2 MARKET MAKERS, SPECIALISTS & LIQUIDITY PROVIDERS

3.2.1 Market Makers

Role: Commit to continuously quoting both buy (bid) and sell (ask) prices for selected securities, profiting from the spread between them.

Function:

- Narrow bid-ask spreads, making it easier for other participants to execute trades with minimal price slippage.

- Absorb temporary order imbalances by buying when supply exceeds demand and selling when demand exceeds supply.

3.2.2 Specialists (Designated Market Makers)

Specific to the NYSE: Each stock is assigned a specialist (now called a Designated Market Maker, or DMM) responsible for maintaining an orderly market.

Function:

- Manage auction openings and closings.
- Step in when trading falls below a threshold to stabilize prices.
- Facilitate large block trades by matching orders or trading from their own inventory.

3.3 ALTERNATIVE TRADING VENUES

3.3.1 Electronic Communication Networks (ECNs)

Definition: Automated systems that match buy and sell orders for subscribers, often allowing after-hours trading.

Benefit: Transparent order books, faster executions, and lower latency for electronic traders.

3.3.2 Dark Pools

Definition: Private venues—often run by broker-dealers or exchanges—where institutional orders can execute anonymously without pre-trade public display.

Purpose:

- Minimize market impact on large orders.
- Preserve confidentiality until after execution.

Considerations:

- Lack of pre-trade transparency can widen spreads on lit exchanges.
- Regulators monitor for conflicts of interest and fair access.

3.4 ORDER ROUTING & EXECUTION ALGORITHMS

Smart Order Routers (SOR):

- Automatically direct orders to the venue offering the best combination of price and speed.
- Weigh factors like displayed liquidity, speed of execution, and historical fill rates.

Execution Algorithms:

- **VWAP (Volume-Weighted Average Price):** Executes orders in line with average market volume to minimize price impact.
- **TWAP (Time-Weighted Average Price):** Distributes trades evenly over a set time period.
- **Iceberg Orders:** Large orders broken into visible "peaks" to hide total interest.

3.5 ROLE OF REGULATORS & OVERSIGHT

3.5.1 Securities and Exchange Commission (SEC)

Mandate: Protect investors, maintain fair and efficient markets, and facilitate capital formation.

Key Responsibilities:

- Enforce securities laws (e.g., Securities Act of 1933; Securities Exchange Act of 1934).
- Oversee disclosure requirements (Form 10-K, 10-Q, 8-K).

- Regulate broker-dealers, registered exchanges, and clearing agencies.

3.5.2 Financial Industry Regulatory Authority (FINRA)

Mandate: Self-regulatory organization for broker-dealers and registered representatives.

Key Responsibilities:

- Write and enforce rules for trading practices, trade reporting, and professional conduct.
- Conduct examinations, enforce compliance, and administer disciplinary actions.

3.5.3 Exchange Self-Regulatory Functions

Each Exchange (NYSE, NASDAQ, etc.) operates its own SRO unit to monitor trading, investigate suspicious activity, and enforce listing standards.

Surveillance Systems: Track patterns of trading that may indicate insider trading, market manipulation, or spoofing.

3.6 CLEARING & SETTLEMENT

Clearing Agencies (e.g., DTC, NSCC): Serve as intermediaries to net buy and sell obligations among participants.

Settlement Cycle (T+2): Standardized timeline ensuring that, two business days after trade date, securities and funds exchange hands—reducing counterparty risk.

Delivery-Versus-Payment (DVP): Settlement method ensuring that securities transfer only if payment occurs simultaneously.

3.7 MARKET STRUCTURE TRENDS & INNOVATIONS

Decimalization: Modern exchanges quote prices in cents rather than fractions, tightening spreads.

Extended-Hours Trading: Pre-market and after-hours sessions allow trading outside traditional 9:30 AM–4:00 PM ET but with lower liquidity and wider spreads.

Regulation NMS (National Market System): Mandates that brokers route orders to the venue offering the best displayed price, fostering inter-venue competition.

Blockchain & Tokenization (Emerging): Experimentation with decentralized exchanges (DEXs) and security tokens promises further evolution of market infrastructure.

3.8 BEST PRACTICES & RECOMMENDATIONS

Know Your Venue: Understand where your broker routes orders—lit exchanges, ECNs, or dark pools—and the implications for speed and transparency.

Consider Execution Quality: Review your broker's published statistics on fill rates, price improvement, and execution speed.

Be Mindful of After-Hours Risk: If you trade extended hours, use limit orders and recognize that liquidity may be thin.

Stay Informed on Regulation Changes: Regulatory reforms can affect trading costs, available venues, and best execution obligations.

Leverage Institutional Insights: Many brokers publish market-structure white papers and execution-quality reports—read them to better understand the mechanics behind your trades.

3.9 KEY TAKEAWAYS

Diverse Participants: Retail and institutional investors, market makers, ECNs, and dark pools all contribute to liquidity and price discovery.

Complex Ecosystem: Smart order routers and execution algorithms determine where and how your orders are filled.

Regulatory Oversight: The SEC, FINRA, and exchange SROs work in concert to enforce fairness, transparency, and investor protection.

Efficient Settlement: A standardized T+2 cycle and clearing-agency netting minimize counterparty risk.

Continuous Evolution: Market structure is dynamic—stay educated on technological advances, regulatory updates, and the emergence of new trading venues.

Armed with a clear understanding of who's who and what's what in today's market structure, you're ready to dive into **Chapter 4: Fundamental Analysis 101** and learn how to evaluate individual companies and their financial health.

4 FUNDAMENTAL ANALYSIS 101

Fundamental analysis involves evaluating a company's financial health, competitive position, and growth prospects by examining its financial statements, ratios, and underlying business drivers. Whereas technical analysis focuses on price and volume patterns, fundamental analysis seeks to determine a stock's "intrinsic value"—the price at which its shares should trade given the company's fundamentals. In this chapter, you'll learn how to:

- Read and interpret the three core financial statements
- Compute and contextualize key valuation and performance ratios
- Build a simple discounted cash-flow (DCF) or earnings-based valuation model
- Recognize qualitative factors that impact valuation

4.1 THE THREE CORE FINANCIAL STATEMENTS

4.1.1 Income Statement (Profit & Loss)

The income statement reports revenues, expenses, and profit over a specified period (quarter or year).

Line Item	Definition
Revenue / Sales	Total amount earned from goods sold or services provided.
Cost of Goods Sold (COGS)	Direct costs of producing goods (materials, labor).
Gross Profit	Revenue − COGS; reflects production efficiency.
Operating Expenses	SG&A (selling, general & administrative), R&D, marketing.
Operating Income (EBIT)	Gross Profit − Operating Expenses.
Interest Expense	Cost of debt financing.
Pre-Tax Income	EBIT − Interest Expense + Other Income.
Tax Expense	Estimated taxes on pre-tax income.
Net Income	Pre-Tax Income − Tax Expense; "the bottom line."
Earnings Per Share (EPS)	Net Income ÷ Weighted-average shares outstanding.

Key Takeaway: Track revenue growth, margin trends (gross and operating), and net-income consistency over multiple periods.

4.1.2 Balance Sheet

The balance sheet provides a snapshot of a company's financial position at a point in time, based on the accounting equation:

Assets = Liabilities + Shareholders' Equity

Assets	Liabilities & Equity
Current Assets	**Current Liabilities**
• Cash & Cash Equivalents	• Accounts Payable
• Marketable Securities	• Short-term Debt
• Accounts Receivable	• Accrued Liabilities
• Inventory	
Non-Current Assets	**Non-Current Liabilities**
• Property, Plant & Equipment	• Long-Term Debt
• Intangible Assets (Goodwill)	
• Investments	**Shareholders' Equity**
	• Common Stock
	• Additional Paid-in Capital
	• Retained Earnings
	• Treasury Stock (negative)

Key Takeaway: A healthy balance sheet features adequate liquidity (current ratio ≥1.5), manageable leverage (debt-to-equity under industry norms), and positive working capital.

4.1.3 Cash Flow Statement

The cash flow statement reconciles net income to actual cash movements, divided into:

Operating Activities: Net Income + Non-cash adjustments (depreciation, amortization) + Changes in working capital (Δ receivables, payables, inventory).

Investing Activities: Cash used for or from capital expenditures (CapEx), acquisitions, asset sales.

Financing Activities: Cash from issuance or repurchase of equity, debt issuance/repayment, dividend payments.

Section	Purpose
Operating Cash Flow	Indicates cash-generating ability of core business operations.
Free Cash Flow (FCF)	Operating Cash Flow − CapEx; cash available for debt/equity holders.
Investing Cash Flow	Shows investment in future growth or divestitures.
Financing Cash Flow	Reflects capital-structure changes and shareholder distributions.

Key Takeaway: Consistent positive free cash flow signals strong underlying business health and funds for dividends, buybacks, or debt reduction.

4.2 KEY RATIOS & METRICS

Ratios distill complex financials into standardized measures for easy comparison across companies and over time. Below are the most widely used categories.

4.2.1 Profitability Ratios

Ratio	Formula	Insight
Gross Margin	Gross Profit ÷ Revenue	Core production efficiency; higher is better.
Operating Margin	EBIT ÷ Revenue	Efficiency of core operations.
Net Margin	Net Income ÷ Revenue	Overall profitability after all costs.
Return on Equity (ROE)	Net Income ÷ Average Equity	How well equity capital is deployed.
Return on Assets (ROA)	Net Income ÷ Average Assets	Efficiency of total asset utilization.

4.2.2 Valuation Ratios

Ratio	Formula	Insight
Price-to-Earnings (P/E)	Share Price ÷ EPS	How much investors pay per dollar of earnings; relative valuation.
Forward P/E	Share Price ÷ Estimated Next-Year EPS	Market's expectations of future earnings growth.
Price-to-Book (P/B)	Share Price ÷ Book Value per Share	Market vs. accounting value of assets; low may indicate value or distress.
Price-to-Sales (P/S)	Market Cap ÷ Revenue	Useful for companies with no earnings.
EV/EBITDA	Enterprise Value ÷ EBITDA	Capital-structure neutral valuation; compares across debt loads.

4.2.3 Leverage & Liquidity Ratios

Ratio	Formula	Insight
Debt-to-Equity	Total Debt ÷ Shareholders' Equity	Balance-sheet leverage; higher implies more risk.
Interest Coverage	EBIT ÷ Interest Expense	Ability to service debt; >3× is generally healthy.
Current Ratio	Current Assets ÷ Current Liabilities	Short-term liquidity; >1.5× is a standard target.
Quick Ratio	(Current Assets − Inventory) ÷ Current Liabilities	Conservative liquidity measure.

4.3 BUILDING A SIMPLE VALUATION MODEL

While comprehensive valuation can employ multi-stage DCFs, a basic model provides a quick sanity check.

4.3.1 Discounted Cash Flow (DCF) — Core Steps

1. **Project Free Cash Flows (FCF)** over 5 years: Base on historical growth rates of revenue, margins, and CapEx.
2. **Choose a Discount Rate (WACC):** Weighted Average Cost of Capital reflects cost of equity and debt, adjusting for capital structure.
3. **Calculate Terminal Value: Perpetuity Growth:** $TV = FCF_5 \times (1 + g) / (r - g)$

Where g is long-term growth (2–3%), r is WACC.

4. **Present-Value Cash Flows:** Discount each year's FCF and terminal value to present using $PV = FCF_t / (1 + r)^t$.
5. **Sum to Enterprise Value (EV):** $EV = \Sigma\ PV(FCF_t) + PV(TV)$.
6. **Equity Value:** Equity Value = EV – Net Debt.
7. **Intrinsic Share Price:** Equity Value / Shares Outstanding.

4.3.2 Earnings-Based Valuation (P/E Approach)

1. **Select Comparable Companies:** Peer group in same industry, similar size and growth.
2. **Determine Median P/E:** Compute P/E for each peer; take the median.
3. **Estimate Target EPS:** Use analyst consensus or your own projection for next-year EPS.
4. **Calculate Implied Value:** Implied Price = Projected EPS × Median P/E.

4.4 QUALITATIVE FACTORS & ADJUSTMENTS

Quantitative analysis must be complemented by qualitative assessment:

- **Competitive Moat:** Brand strength, network effects, regulatory barriers.
- **Management Quality:** Track record, capital-allocation discipline, shareholder alignment.
- **Industry Dynamics:** Growth drivers, cyclicality, regulatory environment.
- **Accounting Adjustments:** Off-balance-sheet items, one-time charges, revenue recognition policies.

4.5 COMMON PITFALLS & HOW TO AVOID THEM

Pitfall	Prevention Strategy
Blindly Relying on One Ratio	Use a suite of ratios to triangulate valuation and performance.
Ignoring Cash Flow in Favor of Earnings	Prioritize free cash flow—earnings can be manipulated by accounting policies.
Overestimating Growth Rates	Base projections on conservative, historically supported growth.
Misapplying Comparables	Ensure peers are truly comparable in geography, size, and business model.
Neglecting Balance-Sheet Health	Always adjust enterprise value for net debt, off-balance-sheet liabilities, and excess cash.
Failing to Stress-Test Assumptions	Conduct sensitivity analysis on discount rates, growth rates, and margins.

4.6 KEY TAKEAWAYS

- **Financial Statements Are Your Foundation:** Master the income statement, balance sheet, and cash flow to understand a company's health.
- **Ratios Simplify Comparison:** Profitability, valuation, leverage, and liquidity ratios help benchmark companies against peers and history.

- **Valuation Is Both Art and Science:** Use DCF for intrinsic-value estimates and P/E multiples for market-based context—always stress-test key assumptions.
- **Qualitative Factors Matter:** Competitive advantages, management quality, and industry trends can justify higher or lower valuations.
- **Continuous Refinement:** Update your models as new data arrives, and always maintain a margin of safety between intrinsic value and market price.

Having established how to evaluate a company's fundamentals and value its shares, you're now ready to explore **Chapter 5: Technical Analysis Basics** and learn how price action and market sentiment interplay with fundamentals.

5 TECHNICAL ANALYSIS BASICS

Technical analysis examines historical price and volume data to forecast future market behavior. While fundamental analysis seeks intrinsic value, technical analysis focuses on patterns and statistical indicators derived from past market activity. This chapter introduces core concepts, chart types, trend analysis, common patterns, and key indicators, equipping you to interpret price action and time your entries and exits more effectively.

5.1 FOUNDATIONS OF TECHNICAL ANALYSIS

Market Psychology

Prices reflect collective emotions—fear, greed, and indecision. Technical tools distill these sentiments into visual patterns and numeric signals.

Price Discounts Everything

All known fundamentals—earnings, news, macro data—are considered "priced in," so the chart itself becomes the primary source of information.

Trends Are Your Friend

Identifying prevailing trends (up, down, or sideways) helps align trades with the market's dominant direction.

History Tends to Repeat

Crowd behavior often creates recurring patterns; technical analysis seeks to exploit these recurring formations.

5.2 CHART TYPES

Chart Type	Description
Line Chart	Connects closing prices over time; offers a simplified view of overall trend.
Bar Chart	Vertical lines showing high, low, open, and close (HLOC) for each period; more detailed.
Candlestick Chart	Colored "candles" representing HLOC; body color or fill indicates directional bias.

Best Practice: Use candlesticks for pattern recognition; switch to line charts for longer-term trend confirmation.

5.3 Trend Analysis

5.3.1 Identifying Trends

Uptrend: Series of higher highs and higher lows.

Downtrend: Series of lower lows and lower highs.

Sideways/Range: Horizontal movement between defined support and resistance.

5.3.2 Drawing Trendlines

Uptrend Line: Connect at least two higher lows; extend forward.

Downtrend Line: Connect at least two lower highs.

Channels: Parallel lines drawn through highs and lows indicating the price "channel."

Tip: The more touches a trendline has without breaking, the more significant it becomes.

5.4 SUPPORT & RESISTANCE

Concept	Definition
Support	Price level where demand overcomes supply, causing price to "bounce" upward.
Resistance	Price level where supply overcomes demand, causing price to stall or reverse downward.
Role Reversal	Once broken, support often becomes resistance and vice versa.

Techniques:

Horizontal Levels: Identify key zones where price has repeatedly turned.

Moving Averages: Dynamic support/resistance (e.g., 50-day or 200-day MA).

Fibonacci Retracements: Ratios (38.2%, 50%, 61.8%) between high and low swings.

5.5 COMMON CHART PATTERNS

Pattern	Description & Implication
Head & Shoulders	Three peaks; middle (head) higher; signals trend reversal when neckline breaks.
Double Top/Bottom	Two peaks (or troughs) at similar levels; indicates exhaustion of trend.
Triangles	Converging trendlines (ascending, descending, symmetrical); often precede breakouts.
Flags & Pennants	Short consolidations after sharp moves; continuation patterns.
Cup & Handle	Rounded base followed by small pullback; bullish continuation signal.

Confirmation: Always wait for a breakout or breakdown with volume confirmation before acting on patterns.

5.6 VOLUME ANALYSIS

Volume as Confirmation:

Rising volume during price advances validates strength; rising volume on declines confirms selling pressure.

Volume Indicators:

On-Balance Volume (OBV): Cumulative measure adding volume on up days, subtracting on down days.

Volume Profile: Distribution of volume across price levels.

5.7 TECHNICAL INDICATORS

5.7.1 Moving Averages

Type	Calculation	Use Cases
Simple MA (SMA)	Average closing price over N periods	Identify trend direction; dynamic S/R.
Exponential MA (EMA)	Weighted to more recent data	Faster response to price changes.

Crossovers:

Golden Cross: Short-term MA crosses above long-term MA (bullish).

Death Cross: Short-term MA crosses below long-term MA (bearish).

5.7.2 Momentum Oscillators

Indicator	Formula Basis	Signal
Relative Strength Index (RSI)	100 − [100 ÷ (1 + RS)], RS = avg up / avg down	Overbought (>70) / Oversold (<30) levels.
Stochastic Oscillator	(Close − LowN) ÷ (HighN − LowN) × 100	Indicates momentum and potential reversals.

5.7.3 Trend & Volatility Indicators

Indicator	Purpose
MACD	EMA(12) − EMA(26) plotted with a 9-day signal EMA; identifies momentum shifts.
Bollinger Bands	SMA ± (2 × standard deviation); gauges volatility and mean reversion.

5.8 TIMEFRAME & MULTI-TIMEFRAME ANALYSIS

Intraday (minutes/hours): For day traders seeking short-term moves.

Daily/Weekly: For swing traders and position traders focused on broader trends.

Multi-Timeframe Approach:

Identify trend on a higher timeframe (e.g., weekly), then refine entries/exits on a lower timeframe (e.g., daily).

5.9 TOOLS & PLATFORMS

Charting Software: TradingView, Thinkorswim, MetaTrader, or broker-provided platforms.

Screeners: Filter stocks by patterns, indicators, volume, and price criteria.

Alerts & Automation: Set price, indicator, or pattern alerts; some platforms allow automated order execution.

5.10 COMMON PITFALLS & MITIGATION

Pitfall	Mitigation Strategy
Over-Optimization ("Curve Fitting")	Avoid back-testing on the exact historical window you intend to trade; stress-test across different periods.
Ignoring Volume	Always confirm patterns and breakouts with corresponding volume spikes.
Chasing Signals	Wait for confirmed closes beyond support/resistance or moving averages.
Repainting Indicators	Use non-repainting tools; be wary of indicators that adjust past signals.
Confirmation Bias	Establish objective trade rules in advance; maintain an honest trade journal.

5.11 BEST PRACTICES & RECOMMENDATIONS

Combine with Fundamentals: Use technical signals to time entries into fundamentally sound stocks.

Define Clear Rules: Pre-specify your entry, stop-loss, and profit-target levels before trading.

Maintain Discipline: Follow your trading plan; avoid impulsive trades on every signal.

Use Risk Management: Limit position size so that no single loss from a stop-out jeopardizes more than 1–2% of your capital.

Continuous Learning: Review key setups weekly; refine your approach based on successes and failures.

5.12 KEY TAKEAWAYS

Charts Reveal Psychology: Price and volume patterns reflect the ongoing tug-of-war between buyers and sellers.

Trend Identification Is Crucial: Align trades with the prevailing trend to improve win rate.

Confirm Patterns with Volume: Volume validates the strength of breakouts and reversals.

Indicators Aid, Don't Replace, Judgment: Use moving averages, RSI, MACD, and Bollinger Bands as complementary tools.

Plan, Execute, Review: A systematic approach—defined rules, disciplined execution, and post-trade analysis—builds consistent edge.

With these technical-analysis fundamentals internalized, you'll be ready to develop a comprehensive investment strategy in **Chapter 6: Developing Your Investment Strategy**.

6 DEVELOPING YOUR INVESTMENT STRATEGY

A well-defined investment strategy guides your decision-making, aligns trades with your risk tolerance and goals, and prevents emotional reactions to market noise. In this chapter, we'll explore common strategic approaches—growth, value, dividend, and passive indexing—examine their characteristics, and provide guidance on selecting and combining strategies to build a portfolio that suits your objectives.

6.1 CLARIFYING YOUR GOALS & RISK PROFILE

Before choosing a strategy, determine:

Time Horizon

Short-Term (≤1 year): Emphasis on liquidity; strategies may include swing trading or sector rotations.

Medium-Term (1–5 years): Blend of growth and income; allows for tactical adjustments.

Long-Term (≥5 years): Focus on compounding; value, dividend, and indexed approaches often excel.

Risk Tolerance

Conservative: Prioritize capital preservation; accept lower returns in exchange for stability.

Moderate: Willing to tolerate some volatility for higher expected returns.

Aggressive: Comfortable with significant drawdowns in pursuit of outsized gains.

Return Objectives

Absolute Returns: Seek positive gains regardless of market direction (may use hedging or market-neutral strategies).

Relative Returns: Aim to outperform a benchmark (e.g., S&P 500) over a cycle.

Document your answers to create an **Investment Policy Statement (IPS)** that outlines objectives, constraints, and permitted strategies.

6.2 GROWTH INVESTING

6.2.1 Definition & Focus

Targets companies with **above-average revenue and earnings growth**, often reinvesting profits to expand.

6.2.2 Characteristics

High P/E Ratios: Investors pay a premium for future growth potential.

Volatility: Prices can swing sharply if growth expectations shift.

Sector Concentration: Often tech, biotech, and high-innovation industries.

6.2.3 Pros & Cons

Pros	Cons
Potential for strong capital gains in bull markets.	Vulnerable to market corrections and overvaluation risks.
Exposure to innovative companies driving secular trends.	Low or no dividends; relies on price appreciation alone.

6.2.4 Best Practices

Use **fundamental screens** for revenue/earnings growth ≥15% YoY.

Employ **stop-loss orders** to guard against sharp reversals.

Limit allocation to a **diversified basket** of 8–12 growth names.

6.3 VALUE INVESTING

6.3.1 Definition & Focus

Seeks companies trading below intrinsic value, often identified by **low multiples** (P/E, P/B, P/S).

6.3.2 Characteristics

Margin of Safety: Purchase price provides cushion against downside.

Dividend Yield: Many value stocks pay dividends, enhancing total returns.

Sector Breadth: Financials, industrials, consumer staples, energy.

6.3.3 Pros & Cons

Pros	Cons
Historically outperform in recovery phases post-bear markets.	"Value traps"—stocks cheap for valid fundamental reasons.
Income potential via dividends.	Can underperform during rapid bull markets led by growth.

6.3.4 Best Practices

Screen for **P/E < industry average** and **P/B < 1.5**×.

Analyze **free cash flow** and **debt levels** to avoid distressed companies.

Combine with **quantitative value models** (e.g., Piotroski F-Score) for quality assessment.

6.4 DIVIDEND INVESTING

6.4.1 Definition & Focus

Prioritizes stocks with **sustainable dividend payouts**, delivering regular income plus potential price appreciation.

6.4.2 Characteristics

Dividend Yield: Annual dividends ÷ share price; typically 2–6%.

Dividend Growth: Companies with a track record of increasing payouts.

Defensive: Many dividend payers are in stable industries (utilities, consumer staples).

6.4.3 Pros & Cons

Pros	Cons
Steady cash flow—sources of passive income.	Yield may compress if interest rates rise.
Downside support—dividends can cushion total returns.	Growth potential may lag non-payers.

6.4.4 Best Practices

Target the **Dividend Aristocrats** (25+ years of increases) for reliability.

Evaluate **payout ratio** (<60% ideal) to ensure sustainability.

Reinvest dividends via **DRIP** (Dividend Reinvestment Plan) for compounding.

6.5 INDEXING & ETFS

6.5.1 Definition & Focus

Passive strategy that tracks a broad market index (e.g., S&P 500) through low-cost ETFs or index funds.

6.5.2 Characteristics

Diversification: Instant exposure to hundreds or thousands of stocks.

Low Costs: Expense ratios often <0.10%.

Market Returns: Delivers benchmark performance less minimal fees.

6.5.3 Pros & Cons

Pros	Cons
Simplicity & discipline—no stock-picking required.	Cannot outperform the market; subject to overall downturns.
Tax efficiency—low turnover reduces capital gains.	Less flexibility to avoid overvalued segments.

6.5.4 Best Practices

Use **broad market ETFs** (e.g., SPY, VTI) as portfolio core.

Consider **sector or factor ETFs** (value, momentum) for tactical tilts.

Automate **periodic contributions** (dollar-cost averaging) to reduce timing risk.

6.6 BLENDED & THEMATIC APPROACHES

Core-Satellite Model:

Core: 60–80% in broad index funds or diversified blue-chips.

Satellite: 20–40% in active strategies—growth, value, dividends, or themes.

Thematic Investing:

Focus on macro trends (green energy, AI, demographics) via specialized ETFs or baskets.

Risk: Concentrated exposures; ensure theme has long-term viability.

6.7 CRAFTING YOUR PERSONAL STRATEGY

Assess Allocation: Divide capital among strategies—e.g., 40% index core, 30% growth, 20% value, 10% dividends.

Define Rules: Set clear **entry/exit criteria**, position-size limits, and **rebalancing cadence** (annual or semi-annual).

Monitor & Review: Track performance relative to benchmarks and your IPS; adjust allocations based on changing objectives or market conditions.

6.8 COMMON PITFALLS & HOW TO AVOID THEM

Pitfall	Prevention Strategy
Overconcentration in One Style	Diversify across multiple strategies to reduce cyclical risk.
Chasing Recent Winners	Stick to your IPS; avoid style drift based on short-term performance.
Ignoring Fees & Taxes	Factor in expense ratios, trading costs, and tax implications when modeling net returns.
Failing to Rebalance	Automate rebalancing or set calendar reminders to maintain target allocations.
Neglecting Psychological Fit	Choose strategies that align with your temperament—don't force aggressive growth if you prefer stability.

6.9 KEY TAKEAWAYS

Strategy Anchors Success: Align your approach with goals, horizon, and risk tolerance, and document it in an IPS.

No One-Size-Fits-All: Combine growth, value, dividend, and passive indexing to create a balanced portfolio.

Discipline & Rules: Predefine allocation, entry/exit, and rebalancing rules to minimize emotional decisions.

Monitor & Adapt: Regularly review strategy effectiveness and adjust in response to life-cycle changes or market regimes.

Stay Educated: As markets evolve, refine your toolkit with new strategies —just ensure they fit within your overarching plan.

With a clear strategy in place, you'll be ready to structure your portfolio and manage asset allocation in **Chapter 7: Portfolio Construction & Management**.

7 PORTFOLIO CONSTRUCTION & MANAGEMENT

Building and managing a portfolio that aligns with your strategic goals, risk tolerance, and time horizon is as critical as selecting individual investments. This chapter covers the principles of diversification, asset allocation frameworks, rebalancing methodologies, and ongoing portfolio oversight to help you optimize returns while controlling risk.

7.1 THE IMPORTANCE OF DIVERSIFICATION

Risk Reduction: Spreading capital across multiple assets reduces the impact of any single security's poor performance.

Smoother Returns: A diversified mix of asset classes often exhibits lower volatility than individual holdings.

Uncorrelated Drivers: Combining assets with low or negative correlations—e.g., stocks and bonds—can improve the portfolio's risk-adjusted return.

Diversification Isn't Just More Names: Simply owning many stocks in the same sector or style provides limited benefit. True diversification spans asset classes, geographies, sectors, and investment styles.

7.2 STRATEGIC ASSET ALLOCATION

7.2.1 Establishing Your Capital Mix

Define Major Asset Classes:

Equities: Domestic large-cap, small-cap, international, emerging markets.

Fixed Income: Treasuries, investment-grade corporates, high-yield bonds, municipal bonds.

Alternatives (Optional): Real estate (REITs), commodities, hedge-fund-style strategies.

Cash & Cash Equivalents: Money-market funds, short-term T-bills.

Match to Risk/Return Profile:

Aggressive: Higher equity weight (70–90%), modest bonds.

Moderate: Balanced split (50% stocks / 50% bonds).

Conservative: Higher fixed-income weight (60–80%), lower equities.

Incorporate Objectives:

Income Focus: Increase bond and dividend-paying stock allocations.

Growth Focus: Overweight high-growth equities, small-caps, and thematic exposures.

7.3 DIVERSIFICATION WITHIN ASSET CLASSES

7.3.1 Equity Diversification

Market Caps: Combine large-cap stability with small-cap growth potential.

Styles & Sectors: Blend growth, value, and quality styles; rotate or overweight sectors by cycle (e.g., technology vs. utilities).

Geography: Allocate to developed foreign and emerging markets to capture global opportunities and mitigate domestic downturns.

7.3.2 Fixed-Income Diversification

Credit Quality: Mix government, investment-grade, and high-yield bonds to balance yield vs. credit risk.

Maturities: Use a ladder or barbell to spread interest-rate sensitivity across short, intermediate, and long maturities.

Inflation Protection: Consider TIPS (Treasury Inflation-Protected Securities) or short-duration real-asset allocations.

7.3.3 Alternative Allocations

Real Assets: REITs or commodity ETFs offer inflation hedges and low correlation with stocks/bonds.

Hedge Strategies: Market-neutral funds or managed futures can provide diversification through non-directional returns.

7.4 TACTICAL ASSET ALLOCATION & TILTS

Tactical Overweights: Short-term deviations (±5–15%) from strategic weights based on market conditions or valuation signals.

Factor Tilts: Add exposure to factors like momentum or quality via specific ETFs or factor funds.

Risk Controls: Use signal thresholds (e.g., P/E above historical average) to trigger tactical shifts.

7.5 REBALANCING YOUR PORTFOLIO

Rebalancing realigns your portfolio to target weights, capturing gains and enforcing buy-low disciplines.

7.5.1 Rebalancing Approaches

Method	Description
Calendar-Based	Rebalance at fixed intervals (e.g., quarterly or annually).
Threshold-Based	Rebalance when an asset class deviates by a set percentage (e.g., ±5%).
Hybrid	Combine calendar checks with threshold triggers.

7.5.2 Benefits & Trade-Offs

Pros:

- Locks in profits from outperformers and redeploys into underperformers.
- Controls drift away from your risk profile.

Cons:

- Transaction costs and potential tax events.
- Over-frequent rebalancing may reduce returns in trending markets.

7.6 PORTFOLIO MONITORING & REPORTING

7.6.1 Performance Metrics

Absolute Returns: Total portfolio return over periods (month, quarter, year).

Risk-Adjusted Returns: Sharpe Ratio, Sortino Ratio, and Information Ratio relative to benchmarks.

Drawdown Analysis: Frequency and magnitude of peak-to-trough declines.

Attribution: Contribution to returns by asset class, sector, or individual holding.

7.6.2 Tools & Dashboards

Portfolio Trackers: Interactive platforms (e.g., Morningstar, individual broker dashboards) to visualize allocations and performance.

Automated Alerts: Threshold breaches, upcoming rebalancing dates, or significant news on key holdings.

7.7 TAX-EFFICIENT MANAGEMENT

Tax-Loss Harvesting: Realize losses to offset gains; reinvest proceeds in similar exposures to maintain asset allocation.

Account Placement: Hold high-yield or tax-inefficient assets in tax-advantaged accounts (IRAs, 401(k)s) and efficient assets (index funds) in taxable accounts.

Dividend Timing: Be mindful of ex-dividend dates and qualified dividend holding periods for favorable tax treatment.

7.8 COMMON PITFALLS & HOW TO AVOID THEM

Pitfall	Prevention Strategy
Under-Diversification	Maintain minimum holdings per asset class; avoid concentration in single names or sectors.
Over-Diversification ("Diworsification")	Limit number of positions to maintain oversight and avoid negligible exposure sizes.
Ignoring Correlation Shifts	Periodically recalculate correlations; adjust allocations as asset relationships evolve.
Emotional Drift	Stick to your IPS; rebalance mechanically rather than reacting to short-term noise.
Excessive Trading Costs	Rebalance considering transaction costs and tax impacts; use cash flows for adjustments.

7.9 BEST PRACTICES & RECOMMENDATIONS

Document Your IPS: Keep a clear policy statement with target allocations, rebalancing rules, and permissible investments.

Automate When Possible: Use automated rebalancing features offered by many brokerages or robo-advisors.

Review Annually: Conduct a formal portfolio review at least once a year to update goals, allocations, and risk parameters.

Leverage Low-Cost Vehicles: Favor ETFs and index funds to implement broad asset-class exposures efficiently.

Maintain a Cash Buffer: Hold a small cash reserve (2–5%) to cover contributions or opportunistic purchases without forcing sales.

7.10 KEY TAKEAWAYS

Asset Allocation Drives Outcomes: The mix of stocks, bonds, and alternatives explains the majority of your portfolio's return variation.

Diversify Thoughtfully: Spread across and within asset classes to smooth returns and manage risk.

Rebalance Disciplinedly: Use calendar or threshold triggers to realign to your strategic weights.

Monitor Performance: Track both absolute and risk-adjusted metrics to ensure alignment with objectives.

Optimize for Taxes: Position assets and harvest losses to keep more of your gains.

Armed with robust portfolio construction and management practices, you are prepared to address risk, behavior, and taxation in **Chapter 8: Managing Risk & Emotions**.

8 MANAGING RISK & EMOTIONS

Successful investing depends as much on controlling risk and one's own psychology as on selecting the right securities. Even the best analysis can be undone by a catastrophic loss or an emotional overreaction. In this chapter, we'll examine:

- Quantitative risk-management techniques
- Position sizing and portfolio-level controls
- Practical stop-loss and take-profit rules
- Behavioral biases that undermine decision-making
- Strategies to maintain discipline and emotional balance

8.1 QUANTITATIVE RISK MANAGEMENT

8.1.1 Setting Risk Limits

Per-Trade Risk

Define a maximum percentage of your capital you're willing to lose on a single trade—commonly 1–2%.

Example: With a $100,000 portfolio and 1% risk limit, you risk $1,000 per position.

Portfolio-Level Risk

Use **Value at Risk (VaR)** to estimate potential loss over a time horizon at a given confidence level (e.g., "2% VaR of $5,000 over 1 day").

Monitor **maximum drawdown**, the largest peak-to-trough decline, and set thresholds (e.g., 10% drawdown triggers strategy review).

8.1.2 Position Sizing

Fixed Fractional Method

Risk a constant fraction (e.g., 1%) per trade.

Position Size = (Account Equity × Risk per Trade) ÷ (Entry Price – Stop-Loss Price).

Volatility-Based Sizing

Larger positions in less-volatile assets; smaller in more-volatile ones.

Use Average True Range (ATR) to gauge volatility and adjust size accordingly.

Kelly Criterion (Aggressive)

Calculates an "optimal" fraction based on win probability and payoff ratio.

Often produces aggressive sizes; many traders use a fraction (e.g., half-Kelly) to curb volatility.

8.2 STOP-LOSS & TAKE-PROFIT RULES

8.2.1 Stop-Loss Orders

Fixed Dollar/Percentage Stop

Exit if price moves against you by a predetermined amount.

Technical Stop

Place stops beyond key technical levels (e.g., below support, trendline, or moving average).

Trailing Stop

Automatically adjust the stop level as price moves in your favor, locking in gains.

8.2.2 Take-Profit Targets

Risk-Reward Ratio

Aim for setups with a minimum 1.5:1 or 2:1 reward-to-risk ratio.

Example: Risking $1 per share to make $2.

Scaling Out

Sell portions of your position at multiple target levels to capture gains while leaving a portion to run.

Time-based Exits

If a position fails to reach profit levels within a set time (e.g., 4 weeks), consider exiting to redeploy capital.

8.3 BEHAVIORAL FINANCE & COMMON BIASES

Investors are human—prone to cognitive errors and emotional swings. Awareness is the first step to mitigation.

Bias	Description	Mitigation
Loss Aversion	Feeling losses more intensely than gains of the same magnitude.	Predefine stop-losses; use automated orders.
Overconfidence	Overestimating one's skill or information edge.	Keep a trading journal; review actual win/loss statistics.
Confirmation Bias	Seeking information that supports a preconceived view.	Deliberately research bearish/contrarian viewpoints.
Anchoring	Relying too heavily on an initial price or reference point.	Base decisions on fresh, relevant data—avoid fixed price anchors.
Recency Bias	Overweighting recent events when predicting the future.	Use longer-term performance records and statistical measures.
Herding	Following the crowd rather than one's own analysis.	Maintain an IPS; question consensus trades and "hot tips."
Regret Aversion	Avoiding decisions to escape potential regret, leading to inaction.	Set clear rules; execute systematic strategies.
Disposition Effect	Selling winners too early and holding losers too long.	Automate exit rules; review holding periods and outcomes.

8.4 MAINTAINING DISCIPLINE & EMOTIONAL BALANCE

8.4.1 Creating a Trading Plan

Pre-Trade Checklist:

Rationale for entry, target price, stop-loss, position size, time horizon.

Document Everything:

Record trades in a journal with emotional state, news catalysts, and strategy used.

8.4.2 Routine Reviews

Daily Review:

Check closed trades, adherence to plan, emotional notes.

Weekly Review:

Analyze performance metrics: Win rate, average win/loss, largest drawdown.

Monthly/Quarterly Review:

Assess strategy effectiveness; update IPS and rules if necessary.

8.4.3 Stress Management Techniques

Set Realistic Expectations:

Accept that losses are part of the process; aim for consistency over one-off big wins.

Mindfulness & Breaks:

Take scheduled breaks from screens; practice breathing exercises or brief walks.

Support Network:

Engage peers or mentors for perspective during challenging streaks.

8.5 CONTINGENCY PLANNING

Emergency Exit Rules:

Predefine market-wide triggers (e.g., S&P 500 drops 5% in a day) to reduce exposure or tighten stops.

Technology Failures:

Maintain backup internet access; know how to place orders by phone.

Account Protection:

Use strong passwords, two-factor authentication, and avoid over-leveraging margin.

8.6 COMMON PITFALLS & HOW TO AVOID THEM

Pitfall	Prevention Strategy
Abandoning Stops Under Pressure	Automate stop orders; never move stops further away to "avoid" a loss.
Over-Trading	Enforce minimum risk-to-opportunity thresholds; follow your trading plan.
Failure to Review Losing Streaks	Conduct post-mortems to identify systematic issues—adjust or pause trading.
Letting Emotions Drive Decisions	Rely on quantitative signals; step away during high-stress or volatile periods.
Neglecting Risk on Winners	Trail stops on profitable positions; realize partial gains systematically.

8.7 BEST PRACTICES & RECOMMENDATIONS

Automate Where Possible: Use limit and stop orders to enforce discipline without needing split-second reactions.

Small Position Sizes: Ensure a losing streak cannot decimate your capital —diversify across trades.

Maintain an IPS: A written Investment Policy Statement holds you accountable to predefined rules and objectives.

Regular Training: Refresh your knowledge of biases and risk techniques periodically.

Leverage Technology: Use portfolio-management tools that track risk metrics in real time (VaR, drawdown, concentration).

8.8 KEY TAKEAWAYS

Risk First: Define and enforce clear risk parameters at both trade and portfolio levels.

Structured Exits: Predefine stop-loss and take-profit rules to manage downside and lock in gains.

Behavior Matters: Recognize and mitigate cognitive biases through plans, journals, and systematic rules.

Discipline Wins: Consistent application of well-tested rules trumps sporadic "gut calls."

Continuous Improvement: Review performance, refine strategies, and adapt to changing market conditions.

With a robust framework for managing both risk and emotion, you're now equipped to optimize your tax and cost efficiency in **Chapter 9: Taxes, Fees & Other Considerations**.

9 TAXES, FEES & OTHER CONSIDERATIONS

Beyond picking stocks and timing trades, savvy investors optimize their net returns by managing taxes and minimizing fees. In this chapter, we'll cover:

- Tax treatment for capital gains and dividends
- Key rules and strategies (e.g., wash-sale, tax-loss harvesting)
- Comparing taxable vs. tax-advantaged accounts
- Brokerage, exchange, and execution costs
- Margin interest and other financing charges
- Recordkeeping and reporting best practices

9.1 TAXABLE VS. TAX-ADVANTAGED ACCOUNTS

Account Type	Tax Treatment	Use Case
Taxable Brokerage	Gains taxed in year realized; dividends taxed when paid	Flexible withdrawals; no contribution limits
Traditional IRA/401(k)	Contributions may be tax-deductible; withdrawals taxed as ordinary income	Retirement savings with upfront deduction
Roth IRA/401(k)	Contributions after-tax; qualified withdrawals (age ≥59½ & 5-year rule) are tax-free	Long-term growth without future tax liability
Health Savings Account (HSA)	Triple tax advantage: deductible contributions, tax-free growth, tax-free medical withdrawals	Medical expenses and supplemental retirement fund

Key Point: Use tax-advantaged accounts for holdings with high expected growth or income to defer or eliminate tax drag.

9.2 CAPITAL GAINS TAXATION

9.2.1 Short-Term vs. Long-Term

HOLDING PERIOD: TAX RATE

Short-Term (≤1 year)

Ordinary income rates (10—37%)

Long-Term (>1 year)

Preferential rates (0%, 15%, 20%) depending on income bracket

Example: A $10,000 gain on a trade held 11 months is taxed at your marginal rate; if held 13 months, taxed at your long-term rate—often 15%.

9.2.2 Wash-Sale Rule

Definition: Disallows a loss on a sale if a "substantially identical" security is repurchased within 30 days before or after the sale date.

Impact: Disallowed loss adds to the cost basis of the new position, deferring tax benefit.

Workaround: Harvest losses using ETFs or non-identical securities to maintain market exposure.

9.3 DIVIDEND TAXATION

Dividend Type	Tax Treatment
Qualified	Taxed at long-term capital gains rates (0%, 15%, or 20%)
Ordinary (Non-Qualified)	Taxed at ordinary income rates

Criteria for Qualified:

- Paid by a U.S. corporation (or qualifying foreign).
- Held the stock >60 days in the 121-day window around ex-dividend date.

9.4 ADDITIONAL TAX CONSIDERATIONS

Net Investment Income Tax (NIIT): Additional 3.8% for high earners on investment income above AGI thresholds.

State & Local Taxes: Vary widely; some states exempt retirement withdrawals or capital gains up to certain amounts.

Tax on Options & Futures: Special rules apply—Section 1256 contracts get 60/40 long-term/short-term treatment.

9.5 BROKERAGE & TRADING FEES

Fee Type	Typical Range	Notes
Commission	$0 (most equities/ETFs)	Some brokers still charge for mutual funds or options.
Exchange/SEC/FINRA Fees	$0.0002—$0.003 per share or round-lot	Passed through to end investors on equity trades.
Bid-Ask Spread	Varies by liquidity (pennies to >$1)	Implicit cost; wider on small-cap or OTC names.
Slippage	0—5% of trade value	Difference between expected and executed price.
Margin Interest	5—10% APR	Charged on borrowed funds; lower rates for higher balances.
Expense Ratios	0.03—1.00% for ETFs; 0.50—1.50% for mutual funds	Ongoing drag on returns; tax-inefficient inside taxable accounts.

9.6 IMPACT ON NET RETURNS

Illustration: A $100,000 portfolio gaining 8% per year but paying 0.50% in fees and 15% long-term tax yields ≈6.3% after costs and taxes.

Takeaway: Even small fee reductions or tax savings compound substantially over decades.

9.7 TAX & FEE MINIMIZATION STRATEGIES

Tax-Loss Harvesting Realize losses to offset gains; reinvest in similar but non-identical assets to maintain exposure.

Asset Location Place high-yield assets (bonds, REITs) in tax-deferred accounts; low-turnover equities in taxable accounts.

Use Low-Cost Vehicles Favor commission-free ETFs and index funds with sub-0.10% expense ratios.

Limit Turnover Reduce realization of short-term gains and associated high tax rates.

Leverage Roth Conversions In low-income years, convert traditional IRA to Roth to lock in tax-free growth.

9.8 RECORDKEEPING & REPORTING

Forms:

- **1099-B:** Reports sale proceeds and cost basis; reconcile to your records.
- **1099-DIV:** Reports dividend income and qualified/non-qualified breakdown.

Cost-Basis Tracking: Ensure broker supports specific identification or average cost methods.

Software & Tools: Use tax-software integrations (e.g., TurboTax, Lacerte) or portfolio-tracking services to automate reporting.

9.9 COMMON PITFALLS & HOW TO AVOID THEM

Pitfall	Prevention Strategy
Triggering Wash-Sale by Accident	Use distinct securities or wait >30 days between loss trades.
Ignoring "Phantom" Fees	Review trade confirmations for exchange, SEC, and broker-surcharge line items.
Misallocating Assets	Follow an asset-location plan; track holdings by account type.
Underestimating Tax Drag	Model after-tax returns, not just pre-tax performance.
Neglecting Year-End Planning	Early December: harvest losses, rebalance, and prepare for expected gains.

9.10 BEST PRACTICES & RECOMMENDATIONS

Integrate Tax Planning Into Strategy: Annual review of realized gains/losses and account balances.

Coordinate with a Tax Professional: Complex situations (estate, business owners) benefit from specialized advice.

Automate Where Possible: Set up regular harvesting and rebalancing via robo-advisors or broker tools.

Monitor Policy Changes: Stay abreast of tax-law updates (e.g., changes to capital-gains rates or deductions).

Keep Detailed Records: Maintain digital archives of trade confirmations, 1099s, and supporting calculations.

9.11 KEY TAKEAWAYS

Taxes & Fees Matter: They can erode 1—2% or more of annual returns—compounding over time.

Use the Right Account: Place tax-inefficient assets in tax-advantaged accounts to defer or eliminate taxation.

Leverage Losses: Tax-loss harvesting and wash-sale awareness preserve benefits.

Minimize Costs: Favor low-cost funds, commission-free trading, and tight-spread securities.

Stay Organized: Accurate recordkeeping and professional coordination ensure compliance and optimize net returns.

With your tax and cost foundation set, you're prepared to explore advanced topics in **Chapter 10: Advanced Topics for Future Exploration** —or, if you haven't yet, revisit **Chapters 1—9** to reinforce core principles before expanding your toolkit.

10 ADVANCED TOPICS FOR FUTURE EXPLORATION

Having mastered the fundamentals—from account setup and analysis techniques to portfolio management and tax efficiency—you may be ready to explore more sophisticated investment vehicles and strategies. This chapter introduces three advanced topics: options trading, short selling, and margin trading. Each offers additional tools to manage risk, enhance returns, or hedge existing positions, but also carries unique complexities and dangers. Use this chapter as a primer; extensive education and practice in simulated environments are essential before committing real capital.

10.1 OPTIONS BASICS

Options are derivative contracts granting the buyer the right—but not the obligation—to buy or sell an underlying asset at a predetermined price before or on a specified expiration date.

10.1.1 Key Terminology

Term	Definition
Call Option	Right to **buy** the underlying asset at the strike price.
Put Option	Right to **sell** the underlying asset at the strike price.
Strike Price	Pre-agreed price at which the underlying can be bought or sold.
Expiration Date	Date when the option contract ceases to exist.
Premium	Price paid by the buyer to the seller (writer) for the option.
In the Money	Call: underlying price > strike. Put: underlying price < strike.
Out of the Money	Call: underlying price < strike. Put: underlying price > strike.
At the Money	Underlying price ≈ strike price.

10.1.2 Basic Strategies

Covered Call

Hold 100 shares long; sell one call option. Generates income (premium) but caps upside.

Protective Put

Hold 100 shares long; buy one put option. Acts as an insurance policy, limiting downside.

Long Straddle

Buy one call and one put with the same strike and expiration. Profits from large moves in either direction.

Vertical Spread

Buy and sell calls (or puts) with the same expiration but different strikes. Defines a range of profit and loss.

10.1.3 Risks & Considerations

Time Decay (Theta): Options lose value as expiration approaches if other factors remain unchanged.

Volatility Sensitivity (Vega): Options premiums rise and fall with implied volatility—both an opportunity and a risk.

Assignment Risk: Writers of American-style options can be assigned at any time, requiring delivery of shares or cash.

Complexity: Payoff diagrams can be non-linear; rigorous scenario analysis is essential.

10.2 SHORT SELLING

Short selling allows you to profit from a decline in a security's price by borrowing shares to sell now and repurchasing them later at a lower price.

10.2.1 Mechanics

Borrow Shares: Arrange via your broker to borrow shares from another account.

Sell Short: Sell the borrowed shares at the current market price.

Cover: Repurchase shares later to return to the lender; profit is the difference between sell and buy prices, minus fees.

10.2.2 Costs & Risks

Margin Requirements: Short positions require collateral—typically 150% of the value of the borrowed shares.

Borrow Fees: Stocks with limited availability may carry high borrow costs.

Unlimited Loss Potential: Unlike long positions (max loss = initial investment), short losses are theoretically infinite as prices can rise without bound.

Short Squeezes: Rapid price spikes can force short-covering cascades, amplifying losses.

10.2.3 Best Practices

Use short selling **sparingly** and only when conviction is strong.

Employ **stop-loss** or **buy-stop** orders to cap losses.

Monitor **borrow rates** and availability continuously.

10.3 MARGIN TRADING

Margin trading involves borrowing funds from your broker to purchase additional securities, potentially amplifying returns but also magnifying losses.

10.3.1 How Margin Works

Initial Margin: Minimum account equity percentage required to open a leveraged position (often 50%).

Maintenance Margin: Minimum equity you must maintain (typically 25–30% of market value).

Buying Power: Amount of capital plus borrowed funds available for trading.

10.3.2 Margin Calls & Liquidation

If equity falls below maintenance levels, brokers issue a **margin call**, requiring deposit of cash or liquidation of positions to restore compliance.

Automatic Liquidation: Failure to meet margin calls can result in forced sales at unfavorable prices.

10.3.3 Benefits & Pitfalls

Leverage: Enhances returns when positions move favorably.

Amplified Risk: Equally amplifies losses, potentially exceeding initial capital.

Interest Costs: Margin loans incur daily interest charges, eroding profitability.

10.4 COMBINING ADVANCED STRATEGIES

Seasoned investors may integrate options, shorts, and margin into comprehensive portfolio strategies:

Hedging Equity Exposure: Use protective puts or collars to limit downside in turbulent markets without entirely exiting positions.

Income Generation: Combine covered calls with high-dividend portfolios to enhance yield.

Arbitrage & Pair Trades: Exploit pricing inefficiencies by simultaneously long and short correlated securities or sectors.

Caution: Complexity grows exponentially when strategies are layered; rigorous modeling, stress testing, and disciplined risk limits are non-negotiable.

10.5 EDUCATION & PRACTICE

Paper Trading: Many brokers offer simulated platforms to practice advanced strategies without real-money risk.

Specialized Courses & Certifications: Consider the Options Industry Council (OIC), the Chartered Market Technician (CMT), or professional seminars for in-depth training.

Mentorship & Communities: Engage with experienced traders or moderated forums to discuss ideas and receive feedback.

10.6 KEY TAKEAWAYS

Understand Before You Trade: Grasp the payoff profiles, risks, and costs of options, short sales, and margin before using them.

Limit Exposure: Allocate only a small portion of your portfolio to advanced strategies until you build consistent proficiency.

Manage Leverage: Whether via margin or derivatives, always define and enforce strict risk limits.

Model Extremes: Stress-test strategies under sharp moves, volatility spikes, and liquidity crunch scenarios.

Continuous Learning: Advanced trading is a lifelong study—stay curious, humble, and disciplined.

While these advanced tools can enhance your investment arsenal, they demand respect and meticulous risk management. As you explore further, always anchor your activities in the core principles outlined in Chapters 1–9.

APPENDIX A: GLOSSARY OF KEY TERMS

A concise, alphabetized list of the most important terms covered in this book, with clear definitions to serve as a quick reference.

A

Active Management An investment approach in which a portfolio manager makes specific security selections and timing decisions to outperform a benchmark index.

Asset Allocation The process of dividing a portfolio across different asset classes (e.g., equities, bonds, cash, alternatives) to balance risk and return.

Average True Range (ATR) A volatility indicator measuring the average range between high and low prices over N periods, used in position sizing and stop placement.

B

Balance Sheet A financial statement at a point in time showing a company's assets, liabilities, and shareholders' equity, based on the equation Assets = Liabilities + Equity.

Bid The highest price a buyer is willing to pay for a security at a given moment.

Bid-Ask Spread The difference between the bid price and the ask price; an implicit cost of trading reflecting liquidity.

Book Value A company's net asset value (total assets minus total liabilities) as reported on its balance sheet, often expressed per share.

Bond A debt security in which an investor lends money to an issuer (government or corporation) in exchange for periodic interest payments and return of principal at maturity.

Breakout A price move above resistance (bullish breakout) or below support (bearish breakdown), often signaling the start of a new trend.

Bull Market A prolonged period of rising stock prices, typically accompanied by strong investor confidence and economic growth.

C

Call Option A derivative giving its holder the right (but not the obligation) to **buy** an underlying asset at a specified strike price before or at expiration.

Capital Expenditures (CapEx) Funds used by a company to acquire or upgrade physical assets such as property, plant, and equipment, deducted when calculating free cash flow.

Capital Gains Profits realized when a security is sold for more than its purchase price. Short-term gains (≤1 year) are taxed at ordinary rates; long-term gains (>1 year) at preferential rates.

Cash Flow Statement A financial statement that reports cash generated and used by a company's operating, investing, and financing activities over a period.

Certificate of Deposit (CD) A time-deposit product offered by banks with a fixed interest rate and maturity date, often used for cash-management and fixed-income exposure.

Chart Pattern A recognizable formation on a price chart—such as head & shoulders, cup & handle, or triangle—that technical analysts use to predict future price movements.

Closed-End Fund An investment company with a fixed number of shares outstanding that trades on an exchange like a stock; distinct from open-end mutual funds.

Correlation A statistical measure (–1 to +1) of how two securities move in relation to each other; used in diversification to combine uncorrelated assets.

Covered Call An options strategy in which an investor holds underlying shares long and sells call options against them to generate income.

D

Debt-to-Equity Ratio Total debt divided by shareholders' equity; a leverage metric indicating the proportion of funding a company derives from debt versus equity.

Derivatives Financial contracts whose value is derived from the performance of underlying assets (e.g., options, futures, swaps).

Discounted Cash Flow (DCF) A valuation method that projects free cash flows over a forecast period and discounts them to present value using a discount rate (WACC).

Dividend A distribution of a portion of a company's earnings to shareholders, typically paid in cash on a regular schedule.

Drawdown The peak-to-trough decline in portfolio or security value, expressed as a percentage, used to measure downside risk.

E

Earnings Per Share (EPS) Net income divided by the weighted-average shares outstanding; a key metric for profitability and valuation (P/E ratio).

Emerging Markets Countries with developing economies and financial markets that offer higher growth potential but also higher political and currency risk.

Ex-Dividend Date The cutoff date on which a stock trades without the next dividend; buyers on or after this date are not entitled to the upcoming payout.

Expense Ratio An annual fee expressed as a percentage of assets that mutual funds and ETFs charge to cover operating costs; directly reduces investor returns.

F

Fibonacci Retracement Horizontal support or resistance lines at key ratios (38.2%, 50%, 61.8%) derived from the Fibonacci sequence, used to identify potential reversal levels.

Free Cash Flow (FCF) Operating cash flow minus capital expenditures; the cash available to equity and debt holders after funding operations and growth.

Fundamental Analysis An investment approach that evaluates a company's intrinsic value by analyzing financial statements, ratios, industry position, and qualitative factors.

G

Gross Domestic Product (GDP) The total monetary value of all goods and services produced within a country in a given period; a key macroeconomic indicator affecting markets.

H

Head & Shoulders A reversal chart pattern featuring three peaks—the middle (head) higher than the two shoulders—signaling potential trend change when the neckline is broken.

I

Index Fund A mutual fund or ETF designed to replicate the performance of a market index (e.g., S&P 500) by holding the same securities in proportion.

Initial Public Offering (IPO) The first sale of company shares to the public, transitioning from private to publicly traded status and raising capital for the issuer.

Insider Trading Buying or selling securities based on material, non-public information; illegal when conducted by corporate insiders outside proper disclosure channels.

Intrinsic Value The perceived "true" worth of a security based on fundamental analysis, which may differ from its current market price.

L

Leverage The use of borrowed capital (margin) to increase the potential return of an investment, also amplifying potential losses and margin risk.

Limit Order An order to buy (or sell) a security at a specified price or better; provides price control but may not execute if the market never reaches the limit.

Liquidity The ease with which an asset can be bought or sold without materially affecting its price; indicated by tight bid-ask spreads and high trading volume.

M

Margin Account A brokerage account in which investors can borrow funds to purchase securities, subject to initial and maintenance margin requirements and interest charges.

Market Capitalization The total market value of a company's outstanding shares: share price multiplied by shares outstanding; used to classify companies as large-, mid-, or small-cap.

Market Maker A firm or individual that continuously quotes bid and ask prices for a security, facilitating liquidity and profiting from the spread.

Moving Average A technical indicator that smooths price data by averaging closing prices over N periods; common types include the simple MA (SMA) and exponential MA (EMA).

O

Over-The-Counter (OTC) Trading of securities not listed on formal exchanges, often via dealer networks; includes small-cap stocks and foreign issues.

P

P/E Ratio (Price-to-Earnings) Share price divided by EPS; assesses how much investors pay for each dollar of earnings, used to compare valuations across companies and sectors.

Portfolio Diversification The practice of spreading investments across asset classes, sectors, and geographies to reduce unsystematic risk and smooth returns.

Premium (Option) The price paid by the buyer of an option contract to the seller (writer) for the right conveyed by the option.

Primary Market Where new securities are issued and sold to investors (e.g., IPOs and follow-on offerings), raising capital for issuers.

R

Resistance A price level at which selling pressure overcomes buying interest, causing price advances to stall or reverse.

Risk-Adjusted Return A performance measure that accounts for the amount of risk taken to achieve returns, commonly using metrics like the Sharpe Ratio.

S

Secondary Market Where existing securities are traded among investors (e.g., on exchanges or ATS), enabling liquidity and price discovery.

Settlement The process by which securities and funds are exchanged after a trade, typically occurring two business days after the trade date (T+2).

Short Sale A strategy that profits from a security's decline by borrowing and selling shares now and repurchasing them later at a lower price.

Spread See "Bid-Ask Spread."

Stop-Loss Order An order to sell a security once its price falls to a specified trigger level, designed to limit potential losses.

Support A price level at which buying interest overwhelms selling pressure, causing a downtrend to pause or reverse.

T

Technical Analysis An investment approach that forecasts price direction by analyzing historical price and volume patterns, indicators, and chart formations.

Total Return The combined return from price appreciation and dividends (or interest), expressed as a percentage of the initial investment.

V

Volatility A statistical measure of the dispersion of returns, often calculated as the standard deviation; higher volatility implies greater risk and wider price swings.

This glossary compiles the essential terminology you'll encounter in Chapters 1–10. Refer back whenever you need a clear, concise definition of the concepts and jargon fundamental to understanding—and succeeding in—the stock market.

APPENDIX B: RECOMMENDED READING & RESOURCES

Below is a curated list of books, websites, tools, and educational programs to deepen your knowledge of the stock market—and to prepare you for our upcoming volumes on options, short selling, and margin trading.

1. Foundational Stock-Market Texts

"The Intelligent Investor" by Benjamin Graham

A timeless primer on value investing, margin of safety, and investor psychology.

"A Random Walk Down Wall Street" by Burton G. Malkiel

An accessible overview of market efficiency, indexing, and behavioral finance.

"Common Stocks and Uncommon Profits" by Philip A. Fisher

Focuses on qualitative analysis and the "scuttlebutt" method of researching companies.

"Security Analysis" by Benjamin Graham & David Dodd

The classic deep dive into balance-sheet and earnings analysis (more advanced).

2. Fundamental & Quantitative Analysis

"Financial Statement Analysis and Security Valuation" by Stephen Penman

Rigorous treatment of accounting adjustments and valuation models.

"Valuation: Measuring and Managing the Value of Companies" by McKinsey & Company

Practical frameworks for corporate-finance professionals.

"Quantitative Value" by Wesley R. Gray & Tobias Carlisle

Combines value screens with statistical techniques for systematic stock selection.

3. Technical Analysis

"Technical Analysis of the Financial Markets" by John J. Murphy

Comprehensive guide to chart patterns, indicators, and market internals.

"Japanese Candlestick Charting Techniques" by Steve Nison

The definitive resource on candlestick patterns and their interpretation.

"Trading for a Living" by Dr. Alexander Elder

Blends technical systems with risk management and trader psychology.

4. Portfolio Management & Risk

"Asset Allocation: Balancing Financial Risk" by Roger C. Gibson

In-depth exploration of strategic and tactical allocation across asset classes.

"The Intelligent Asset Allocator" by William Bernstein

A concise guide to modern portfolio theory and practical diversification.

"Against the Gods: The Remarkable Story of Risk" by Peter L. Bernstein

Narrates the evolution of risk measurement and its application to finance.

5. Behavioral Finance & Psychology

"Thinking, Fast and Slow" by Daniel Kahneman

Groundbreaking insights into cognitive biases that affect investor behavior.

"Nudge: Improving Decisions About Health, Wealth, and Happiness" by Richard H. Thaler & Cass R. Sunstein

Explores how small design changes can "nudge" better choices.

"Misbehaving: The Making of Behavioral Economics" by Richard H. Thaler

A lively account of how irrational behavior reshapes economic theory.

6. Tax & Cost Optimization

"Tax-Efficient Investing: A Guide to Reducing Your Tax Burden" by Joseph M. Rosen

Practical strategies for asset location, harvesting, and retirement-account planning.

Brokerage Platforms with Tax Tools

Vanguard and **Schwab** offer built-in tax-loss harvesting for eligible accounts.

Wealthfront and **Betterment**: robo-advisors with automated harvesting and asset-location features.

7. Online Learning & Communities

Investopedia (www.investopedia.com)

Detailed articles, tutorials, and video explainers on virtually every financial topic.

Coursera & edX

Yale's "Financial Markets" (Robert Shiller)

Wharton's "Introduction to Corporate Finance"

Community Platforms

Seeking Alpha & StockTwits

Platforms for market commentary, idea sharing, and community discussion—exercise discernment.

r/investing, r/stocks, r/financialindependence (Reddit)

Peer-to-peer forums; use moderators' flair and upvotes to vet advice.

8. Software & Data Tools

Charting & Screening

TradingView: Advanced charting with community scripts.

Finviz: Free stock screener with heat maps and fundamentals.

Portfolio Trackers

Personal Capital: Integrates all accounts, shows allocation and performance.

Morningstar Portfolio Manager: Robust analytics and attribution.

Back-testing & Quant Platforms

QuantConnect, **Backtrader**: Python-based frameworks for strategy simulation.

AlgoTrader, **MetaTrader**: Commercial platforms for algorithmic trading.

9. Preparing for Options, Short Selling & Margin

To get a head start on our upcoming volumes:

"Options as a Strategic Investment" by Lawrence G. McMillan

Deep reference on options strategies, payoffs, and Greeks.

"Option Volatility & Pricing" by Sheldon Natenberg

Advanced treatment of volatility, modeling, and risk management.

"Short Selling: Strategies, Risks, and Rewards" by Frank Fabozzi & Roland Fuss

Comprehensive guide to mechanics, regulation, and risk controls.

"Margin of Trust: A Trader's Guide to Margin" (O'Reilly / online tutorials)

Articles and courses explaining margin rules, interest, and forced liquidations.

10. Podcasts & Video Channels

"We Study Billionaires" (The Investor's Podcast Network)

Interviews with top investors on strategy and psychology.

"Chat With Traders"

In-depth conversations with active traders across markets and instruments.

YouTube Educators

Rayner Teo: Technical-analysis tutorials.

Aswath Damodaran: Valuation lectures from NYU Stern.

Next Steps: As you explore these resources, maintain focus on your Investment Policy Statement and apply new insights systematically. When we launch our follow-up titles on options, short selling, and margin trading, you'll already have the foundational knowledge—and the context—to dive deeper with confidence.

ABOUT THE AUTHOR

Dr. Alhaji K. Tarawally is an expert in international relations, communications, event management, and migration issues. He focuses on addressing Africa's brain drain and the impact of global immigration policies. His initiatives, such as the "African Talent Retention Initiative" and the "Global Migration Policy Reform Proposal," reflect his extensive cross-cultural experiences. Dr. Tarawally has consistently advocated for sustainable development, youth empowerment, and equitable migration frameworks to combat talent loss from the continent.

Dr. Tarawally holds advanced degrees from prestigious institutions around the world. He earned a Ph.D. in International Relations from Selinus University in Italy, which is affiliated with California University FCE. He also has a master's degree in International Relations from Schiller International University in Germany and another from the University of Roehampton in England. Additionally, he holds a B.A. Honours Degree in Mass Communication and a Peace and Conflict Resolution Diploma from Fourah Bay College, University of Sierra Leone. These qualifications give him a comprehensive global perspective on international relations, development communication, and migration dynamics.

Dr. Tarawally's significant contributions have earned him international recognition, including the 100 Most Influential African Youth Leadership Award and the National Media Personality Award. He was also named one of the 100 Most Inspiring Sierra Leoneans. His role as a youth ambassador for the Pan African Youth Leadership Foundation and the Sierra Leone Ministry of Youth Affairs is a testament to his commitment to promoting youth empowerment, good governance, and diaspora engagement, inspiring hope for the future.

As a published author and esteemed university lecturer, Dr. Tarawally is at the forefront of advocating for the reform of immigration policies to mitigate brain drain. His critical insights inspire positive change, educate and inform, and empower future generations across Africa and beyond.

www.ingramcontent.com/pod-product-compliance
Lightning Source LLC
LaVergne TN
LVHW022309200926
848481LV00004B/1254